The Mizzy

Paul Farley

The Mizzy

PICADOR

First published 2019 by Picador
an imprint of Pan Macmillan
The Smithson, 6 Briset Street, London EC1M 5NR
Associated companies throughout the world
www.panmacmillan.com

ISBN 978-1-5290-0979-8

3 5 7 9 8 6 4 2

A CIP catalogue record for this book is available from the British Library.

Printed and bound by CPI Group (UK) Ltd, Croydon, CR0 4YY

Visit **www.picador.com** to read more about all our books
and to buy them. You will also find features, author interviews and
news of any author events, and you can sign up for e-newsletters
so that you're always first to hear about our new releases.

This book is for Tim Dee

Contents

Starling   1

Atlas   2

Poker   3

Accumulator   4

Goldcrest   5

Glorious Goodwood   6

Clever and Cold   7

Lark and Linnet   8

The Ship in the Park   9

The Mystery   10

Glade   12

Song Thrush   13

Water Nymph at a First Generation Magnox Storage Pond   14

Gentian Violet   16

Robin   17

The Green Man   18

Moorhen   19

Bananaquits, St Lucia   20

The Sloth   21

Critique of Pure Reason   26

Lunula   27

The Gadget   28

The Keeper of Red Carpets   30

Entry, 1981   31

Life During the Great Acceleration   33

Moss   34

Sparrowhawk   35

Adrenaline   36

Long-Eared Owl   37

Nightjar   42

Panic Attack, Tsukiji Market   43

Mistle Thrush   45

Hole in the Wall   47

Swing   48

Curlew   50

The Story of the Hangover   51

Positioning   52

Oiks   53

Treecreeper   55

Quadrat   56

Gannet   58

Saturday   59

Great Black-Backed Gull   61

Beach   62

Acknowledgements   65

The Mizzy

Starling

All I've ever done with my life
is follow the average course of the crowd
and witter on about my hole in the wall,
the place where I'm from, to any bird that would listen.

Ask anyone. They'll all say the same.
Did he speak of his wall time, his time in the hole?
All through the winter gathering and roost
I spin my line. Others do the same.

All I've ever done with my life
is steer a flight among an old swarm
and soon I'll be dead and the swarm will go on,
so thanks for allowing one starling a voice

but if I 'brood in my hole in the wall'
and 'keep one eye on the summer stars
viewed as from the bottom of a well',
well, that's only you in your human dark.

[1]

Atlas

It wasn't a globe, it was the whole starry heavens,
but before I was sent to stand in the west
with the weight of the sky on my back
I did lift the northern hemisphere
and opened the equator a crack,
carefully, so the bottles inside
didn't quake, for fiery swigs.
Clan Dew. Bristol Cream.
The world tilted, then
I closed the lid,
gigantic.

Poker

You're told this deck was found
in some shattered bothy or croft
north of the Great Glen,
missing its six of diamonds,
shuffled and dealt to a soft
pliancy, greased with lanolin

and you're told this deck lived behind
the bar in a barracks town
and came out to play most nights,
cut between the Falklands
and Iraq, its spring long gone,
dark-edged with mammal sweat

and you're told this deck is the one
recovered from a halfway house
where fatty stalactites
grew in a microwave oven,
where a bottle of Famous Grouse
was brandished in a fight

and it might be a pack of lies
or it might be a sleight of hand,
and you can't tell which is a bluff
because words are a good disguise
for holding nothing. I've found
that nothing is more than enough.

Accumulator

To think of him studying the form
on a Saturday morning, his close reading
of the racing pages,
                    the long hour
when we know better than to disturb him,

and to think of how it could be poems
he pores over, anything that adds
to the stock of available reality,

raw lyrics in the horses' names,
the found poetry of lists; to think of him

caught in this huge attention; outside,
a world begins beyond our gate;

the letterbox holds its breath, the furniture
stands its ground, the bailiffs wait,

and this spell he casts
                    makes nothing happen
though sometimes all our silences
and heavy going are rewarded

when every door in the house yawns open
then slams in an unbroken sequence.

Goldcrest

The penny drops. You've only ever *heard*
the goldcrest, till you find one in a mist net
and the ringers show you how to handle a bird
not much bigger than a bumble bee—
who'd notice if you slipped it in your pocket
like a coin they use to balance up the scales?
Blown through starlight on an easterly gale
you weigh the Baltic States and the North Sea,
arrived from euro airspace into sterling
to circulate among the highest treetops
where they live right on the edge of human hearing,
and as we age and money comes to seem
the simple trap we fall into to dream
our days away . . . Just then the music stops.

Glorious Goodwood

Saturday. Under orders. Just before the house
turned upside down, just before the bites and stings
of horseflies, just before the hooves' cadence,
a rise and fall that lasted about a minute.
There being only that, and no seeing beyond it.
A plague on our house, living from moment
to moment, blinkered down to a few furlongs,

then we were away, all gone, his mad dance
that could fill a house with silence or song
recorded only here, the television's
fever broken, the house itself, all gone
while his horse is still running and the horseflies
still out for blood and in my blood, as once
forty years ago, up North on the South Downs.

Clever and Cold

It's hard being clever and cold.
And I should know. Jack Frost came
to my childhood window one night and told
me: *Look, from now on things won't be the same.*

Its great stillness is not merely a pose.
Not coming in from the cold, but cold coming in.
I try to keep warm but ever since
our little mind-to-heart, I've known
cold's wider intelligence.

How all days should be crystal days.
You can see cold for yourself at work
in the shapes it makes
out of any January park:
fangs on the lip of the slide; a lid for the lake.

The sky is thinking hard before it snows.
You can see how frost hides from the sun,
keeping itself to the shadows
of walls and hedges. It has a mind of its own.
The sun can't have everything its own way.

These are some of the things cold knows.

Lark and Linnet

So it happens the sun
                 and the tilt of the train
and a smell like stone drying
       and a faint song playing
align, and we're back again
                 walking the Lanes
         towards the Park
      we enter through old iron gates

and though it takes the bite
             of planetary gears
     to place me here, the weight
of years,
        I've learned it's also light
    as air   and how to hold it
     is to be held, until
given names, it disappears.

The Ship in the Park

Most parks harboured one, an inland mooring
but we don't know that yet. This one is ours.
Skeletal steel, a biro or a blueprint
of a ship from central casting, drawing
the kids who've tired of the swing or spent
hours behind the wheels of burned out cars.

Galleon style. Old Spice. On a tide of tarmac
glittering with broken glass—as if some giant
bottle had been smashed and the ship slipped free
but couldn't set sail from this dry dock—
a playground wind blew straight through it; a crescent
moon rose with no influence on this sea.

England's Glory. We climb its empty frame
and fight over who's captain. One keeps lookout.
The white flats loom like icebergs. A sheet of rain
twitches with sharks. Deep in a half term's doldrums
we lie down in its hull like cargo, start
to smoke, or learn to drink Lamb's Navy rum

and puke over the side. We ran aground
like that. The Cutty Sark. The Marie Celeste.
The Hispaniola. The Bounty. The Onedin Line.
All the ways we found to live and play in the past
on a riveted-to-the-spot, spot-welded sign
abandoned in a few moons, lost with all hands.

The Mystery

There's a funfair in the small bones of my ears.
It's pitched up in the deep olfactory bulb,
in the crosshairs of my eyes. It lights the marrow
of my long bones, with a hoop for every year
it turned this park into a diamond district,
each slow excited stride from ride to shy
beyond the goldfish that would grow a bib
of mould in time, beyond the smell of straw
and caramel and two-stroke generators.
Even the big wheel still turns inside me,
though the thing itself has long since gone for scrap,
and every bulb's blown to an iron-grey dust.

You must still hang there in the moving night,
unaware this blank machinery
is doing such dark work, until a slight
catch in the throat and shiver passing through
which we call déjà vu. A thought like that
can swing one of two ways: either you feel
yourself the very centre of all things—
the girls laughing, the cinder toffee, the bulbs
like hot rivets holding the dusk around you—
or you can feel the cold all of a sudden,
a mouse inside a town hall clock's movement
frozen before the iron strike of the hour,

and all at once the fluke, the joke, of being alive
lies open and exposed, a sheet-steel sky
shutting the furnace door on Wavertree,
the spoke that holds him pointing towards nothing,
an axle groan rising above the music.
And so he hangs there in the moving night,
knowing the big wheel has to set him down,
a stop/start through fifteen degrees of arc;
that the man who took his money will take his hand
like any boatman would; but he stays aboard
a while longer, for one more go around,
and leaves me standing in an empty park.

Glade

From the long loan book of recurring dreams,
the one where I'm opening the library
on Ladbroke Grove, entering the alarm
code, letting off a chain of lights,
making up a float, chasing out the cold

and a ring of chairs in a cove among
the shelves where I set fresh papers out
then shake a can of air freshener
and hang a mist in the air. I draw
the bolt and wedge open the door

and in they come. They've got no faces
any more, but their clothes are pigeon,
stock brick, plane bark, pavement greys.
They make a bee-line for certain chairs
and are surely most of them dead these days

but here they're still studying furiously
as I guard the peace—I'm the one who's asleep,
remember—from headlines to small print shares.
The silence deepens. The world turns.
I've never been happier in my work.

Song Thrush

One used to perch on its anvil
under the currant bush
in the corner of our yard, a

shady spot where we'd watch it bash
a snail like its gavel
and leave a broken home.

This stone was about the size
of an old dial telephone,
and sometimes the bird would stop,

snail still in beak,
and tilt its head to one side
as if it were listening into the shell,

as if it were a receiver that said
something back,
something so outrageous or stupid

it wanted to telegraph the fact
to us, a technique
students are taught at RADA,

a way to react
so we'd be able to tell
the caller had suddenly hung up.

Water Nymph at a First Generation Magnox Storage Pond

We hook up in the last places you'd look.
Flooded subways, lift well pools
where rain holes up, gazed-over gravelled shallows,
moss gardens on bus stop shelter roofs:

we're found near waters just like these since Zeus
got us on zero hours contracts,
having deserted springs, dew ponds and tarns,
taken our severance, joined the queues
and tell our sob stories of meres and fens
long drained, filled in, paved over,

cry me a river. Some babble: new reservoirs
will create thousands of jobs; purists
sit on their arses, waiting for water features
to come to them. But if they'd take a cistern,

a temporary post beside a rain butt,
a bath plumbed into quickset for the cattle,
a leaky fridge condenser, hoof print, divot
or—sod it—a puddle, there's always work to be had.

Lately in the kingdom of the blind
they've built these radioactive oubliettes
—keeping the lights on means having to forget—

and after two millennia of mills,
of aqueducts and sullen moats,
we gather in their background shine. Those clicks
are the echolocation of exiled nymphs.

Listen to this one. A century of gutters.
That one got stuck next to a dead man's kettle.
Another slummed it by a whirlpool spa for years.
If you're picturing pale skin and golden tresses,

my hair falls out in tufts. Maybe we're turning mortal
from bathing alongside scrapped fuel rods,
old thunderbolts rusting and spent,
where water carries a charge and taste

like coins banked in a civic fountain's silt,
or—this is going back—pools with the taint
of lead scrolls scratched with binding spells or curses.
Words that would burn in air.

In this lido left to stagflate, I need only apply
myself to my reflection and there's a post
for life, longer than a life: no wishes or spite
can outlast all this legacy sludge.

I'm inventorying the waste, just like I used
to count the flowering grasses
and clouds that lingered in those earliest springs
before I watched a world evaporate.

Gentian Violet

Finding a roadside gentian activates
a sunset clause in the laws of common sense:
as I'm about to nick it from this verge
the flower sends a little shock to my hand.
The rainbow runs to earth: beyond here
it's all geophysics, worms, Pluto's blue torch
in the body-scan, where flowers are the wounds
they once were gathered to heal, it's a certain stain
in a sweetheart deal with bees, cut-flower scents
during the night feed on a ward, it's the vein
that rises for a moment in your breast.
Now the flower blooms harder, the way a fire
in a city, seen from air support, shorts out
a block or two of power around itself
and cultivates more dark to flare against.

Robin

It's not so much that robins follow us
more like they lead the way, going on ahead
like useless guides with not one word of our language
but fluent in flow and lode, flitting along
whichever way we walk, breaking into song

before we catch up, and they're off again, a few yards
further into the future. We love them for this,
for spelling it out, for showing us where the edge
of the present moment is.
                     A breeze has shook
the holly or whitethorn and the robin has gone,
leaving me on the sky-puddled tarmac
straddling the powerlines, along the Black Path
that forked under a streetlamp, beside the White Bridge
where the open fields began and the smell of earth
was strong.
              I've stood in all of these places
and a part of me stands there still, till a robin surfaces
and I follow it out, as I did then. Robin, lead on.

The Green Man

The boy who taught us how to charm the worms
by throwing Fairy Liquid on the grass,
then how to bait our hooks and cast a line
into the pool where little perch would rise,
who knew the Vulcan pinch and the Cruyff turn,
who whistled with his thumb and forefinger,

who understood how damp and sappy wood
burned slowly with a yellowy-green flame,
who showed us how to slap life from a fish,
who knew that hogweed bled a poison sap,
who taught us how to bluff at stud poker,
who told ghost stories in a broken whisper,
who took the first watch and the only watch,
who left the tent at dawn to steal the milk,

has been kicked to death in the car park of a pub
on the other side of the year two thousand,
a land we liked considering at length,
the things we'd do in it and who we'd be,
before we fell asleep while he stood guard
as the fire died and the stars formed up above.

Moorhen

Shy, maternal, unknowable
haunter of water edges, bearing a red
shield like a cross. There is no danger here.

Primitive three-pronged claw
designed for the packed mud and its sheen
of algae: a print from central casting.

Prey-bird in your forest of reeds,
a few scene-changes from being flightless,
you could walk back there again.

And why stop there?
Keep going, little moorhen.
You carry in your heart the code

to scale up, to sprout true teeth,
to rise with the ruby eyes of a dinosaur
from the lake where we hire boats by the hour.

Bananaquits, St Lucia

Floods and landslides block the airport road.
Bridges are down. We're greeted by a bird
that urges us to *quit*.
                              Then days of firsts:
flying fish, twilights that fade in seconds,
a table laid with water pistols to squirt
any finch that rocks up thinking it's Bede's sparrow.

The Palm House in the Park gets off the ground
easily, a wrought iron memory palace
filled with light, where I'd sleep under glass
in my pram during winter opening hours,
or so the story goes.
                              A hummingbird
that doesn't know the words docks with a flower.
This is only a flying visit. We leave tomorrow.

The Sloth

cold vision
Will have no counterfeit
Palmed off on it.
            —Sylvia Plath

From the Deadwater Fell transmitter, a long walk down
        towards the lake through planted slopes,
through stacked birthyards of timber sown
    in groups
    of Norway Spruce, Greek Fir, Scots Pine
        neat as new towns, down quiet avenues
            of firebreaks, stitched by the pitchy whine
of chainsaws—close by/far off: hard to say—
        and after walking miles, through many years
            of unclimbed heights and pillared depths, the day
has dropped its guard and a figment hangs in plain view

stopping you in your tracks. Either this is interference
        from television (that bad medium
and fate for beasts like sloths that chance
    their arm
    quietly and in slow motion:
        to be chopped up in a forest of fast editing),
            or you are channelling a specimen
        from an underfunded regional museum
        where keepers tried to carefully compose
            a dead tree's dioramic universe
and there, arranged about its height and root and span

other once-living things—from a dual carriageway of ants
    whose columns raised the tall standards
of leaves, to the windless canopy's haunts
  for birds
  pinned into attitudes of song—
    coincided as they never did in their days
      or damp, electric nights. The whole display
    could be viewed on two levels, so divided
    species. You'd wonder: was it the same for us,
      if those who gazed from the lower deck of the bus
that brought them loved the leafmould, where scarcely a ray

of skylight reached, and slowly the jaguar would appear
    and then by following its eyes
into a deeper shade, the shy
  tapir;
  hunter and quarry tightly bound
    in the coiled spring before the pounce and cry
      that never came, an outcome undecided
    so all the stronger impressed in a mind
    drawn to the dark. Others preferred to wander
      up serpentine stairs, past the fronds and vines
of the understory, true home of houseplants, the anaconda

that shivered the perpendiculars into life,
    where, at the end of a short climb
into this world of bough and limb
  and leaf,
  you'd find the sloth. You'd think: *The sloth!*

It smiled back, always a model of good grace
      in its airy offices, grateful for each throng
of gazes crowded in its field of vision.
It read your minds. *I'd shinny up and hang*
      like that, given half a chance . . . Seeing the face
of a classmate cloud with the facticity of its former being

could blow-dart this: *That sloth's got sawdust in its skull –*
      Still, it thrived beyond the elements
where no sap rose and no rain fell
   which meant,
   next to the plasticized tree toad,
      the Spanish moss, the monkey with the eyes,
         and the tree itself, as rootless as a flag pole,
      it became the quickest creature in this jungle.
      Stared at long enough, you'd swear its mouth
         suppressed a steady deepening, a grin
returned, with interest, and slowly you came to realize

how those shirt-hanger toes were moving by degrees
      (you used to take magic on trust)
around the clock-face of the tree
   and crossed
   the shiny, equatorial bark
      by increments the adults couldn't see.
         What an afterlife. To hang there, upside down
      in another hemisphere. After the moist
      and rich rafters of the Atlantic Forest,
         the journey home seemed drab and undershadowed.
Years passed. Time lapsed. Some kind of slow ingress or drain

meant every pilgrimage to this land of zero growth
    grew less revered, until you shot
a glance so quick that you forgot
    the sloth
    soon as you re-entered the day,
        while it listened to rain drumming on the skylight
            during unvisited hours, the short-cased tick
      of museum beetles, the totem pole's dull cracks
      as the building cooled. Downstairs, the jaguar laid
        his long ambush. All lived their second lives
like that, far longer than their firsts. Until, one night,

a fire burned the roof off that world, and the rain
      —for the first time since time stopped—
beaded its fur. The sloth was trapped
    again
    and cast to star on a ghost train
      as Pan (unbilled); singed, motheaten, bent
        upright, an interior gargoyle set to pounce
    on paying passengers like you, who went
    and saw, among the skeletons and bats,
      the sloth, caught in a flash, just like it once
appeared to a troop of sheltering monkeys in the light

of an ancient storm. Your childhood wasn't properly earthed:
    the carefully curated tree,
the ghost train in its tented fair
    were free
    to flicker into life, or fall
      from view, every discarnate spectacle

and image creeping to some further lair
like this, where the biomass retires to lick
its wounds. Sitkas and larch tower in their dark
postwar vertical hold, silent and still,
and you catch up with yourself. Neither hide nor hair

of the sloth has been seen in years, but this forest you stand
inside is a kind of mind, the rain
its cold vascular system, planned
to drain
into a manmade lake or climb
the living wood to meet itself in time
on the ends of needles, dendrites, pineal
seed cones human eyes will never see,
where a shy dryad has found a place to dwell
high in the branches of its modal tree
and refuses to have anything to do with you again.

Critique of Pure Reason

Who hasn't thought of two raindrops
that, by some hydrostatic fluke,
fall side by side the whole way down?
And talking to one another, too!
Like skydivers before they pull
the cord lip-read, except raindrop falls
are graceful, free from all the roar
of air—this being what they were made for.
What conversations to imagine,
though there's scant time to get beyond
pleasantries, chit chat, the weather,
and seeing as this won't happen again
their talk turns urgent, to the point.
Entering the last hundred feet
through a broken pane in a station roof
or towards a road japanned with rain
or the opened chute of a sycamore
is an ecstasy of parting—*Be good.*
I doubt I'll see you anytime soon—
and at this point the daydream stops
and raindrops stop being raindrops.

Lunula

after Yakuo Tokuken

The moon curves through its million-mile course . . .
You can spot the weirdos a mile away,
telling us how its orbit strays
from earth at the speed a fingernail grows.

The Gadget

An algorithm yoked to a smart microphone
means it can throw my voice. (Years ago, this meant
the cutting out of a comic book coupon
down the dotted line, a postal order sent
to a PO Box on the Avenue of the Americas
where every handshake buzzed and sea monkeys swam;
on the wing and a prayer of knowing what a 'zip code' was,
in the hope the whole thing wasn't an elaborate scam.)
Is that me, trapped in the anchorhold of a post box?
Is that me, in my own pocket, on ringtone?
This is more fun than black soap or x-ray specs.
I laugh on the edge of the centre of attention.

But the gadget can be serious and tactical.
It can throw a thousand lumens and singe eyebrows.
It ships with an optional anodized strike bezel
and defends itself with an avian shrill that could 'rouse
Saint Michael the Archangel's flapping host'
according to the literature. More practical
perhaps is the way it calculates how lost
I'd be without it, and chirrups reminders, missed calls.
I'd tell you its name, but then you might guess my password.
I'd tell you its name, but it won't recognize your voice.
If found, it will thrum in your hand like a frightened bird
as it arms itself and becomes a small device.

Can yours do this? Positioned at my temple
its alchemic palladiums and golds
excite me, bringing pleasure. Or, with a simple
click it can open a vein in spring lancet mode.
Box of sobs, bearer of pipesmoke, putty,
the inkiness of a comic read by torchlight,
it can dowse a water main in the darkest city,
and I've wondered if it feels me feeling sorry for it;
this thing that fits in my hand but can never outlive me,
this thing that sulks on standby facing the iron pole
of the planet, that knows my blood type and search history.
It points towards the presence of a soul.

The Keeper of Red Carpets

Come in. Please be careful. Mind your step.
He keeps them in the dark.
It stinks, I know. Like a stable or a paddock.
Perspective slackens like an ankle rope

in a gallery. Carpets sleep off the world,
digesting its flash and glamour,
its royal visits and movie premiers.
He's dragged last night's returns in, tired and soiled,

to see to their cigarette burns, studs of gum.
Always the indents of heels:
money's bitemarks leave a trail.
A few lie about—unfiled—like ruin columns.

Armed with a dandy brush he settles them down
with a beating and a groom,
and talks to them when the stain removal fumes
fuddle him and make his eyes run.

Safe now from so much as a glance,
he sleeps among them in the racks.
The stockroom phone is ringing off the hook.
Somebody's always looking to make an entrance.

Entry, 1981

There must be catacombs, bone shops,
potters' fields, barrows, plague pits
that contain the only record of lives
lived—no cuneiform, glyph, or notch
on a stick, in clay, to mark they came
this way, got taxed, dwelt here, did that—
those who escaped paper and ink
to leave their traces downriver
in blood, colostrum, marrow. So,

to discover we had personal data
was a big deal that April. School hours,
when anything that broke the humdrum
was welcomed—somebody bringing in
a piece of Skylab, the x-ray van, a poet
in class—or the Careers Officer
who pitched up in the sickbay. Summoned
from History, we formed a queue
to have our fortunes told. His machine

shuffled and riffled—blackjack inside
a tumble dryer—our aptitudes
and details matched at dizzying speeds
to a shrinking sector called utopia,
and five minutes later dealt our cards.

The Careers Officer had other schools
to visit, and many more predictions
before sundown. I've a memory now
of him pulling a plastic shroud over
his big machine, bossing around
the two caretakers who lugged it out
like a mandarin's sedan, with him
leading his own procession, a man
whose card was marked but didn't know it.

Life During the Great Acceleration

I was a data furrier. After mink came sable.
The two escaped and ran down the same cable.

I was a datafarrier. I shod the switchers
that galloped on the spot in air-cooled pastures.

I was a data cooper, a hooper of light:
gallons, firkins, barrels and hogsheads of bytes.

I was a data monger. I sold your histories
to the highest bidder among disinterested third parties.

I was a datafettler, defragger of drives,
a grinder of rough edges, a filer of lives.

I was a datacollier and went down the pit.
At the end of each shift I was strip-searched for pixels or bits.

I was a data tanner. I lifted your skin
while it was still blood-warm with information.

Moss

At the junction where The Wrong Side of the Tracks
meets Memory Lane   where the mighty sodium mast
looks down on everything from a kestrel's height
      as the cutting passes through the fossil record
and filed horizons   where sandstone turns the green
of a sea wall   ferns the green of a banker's lamp
beyond Broad Green   where we trespass on the line
and put our ears to the rail like they did in films
      where an Iron Age head listens to the party wall
of a pond   where thrown-back carp bask in their status
and all are shaken by timetable   where the moon
fits the description of the smoked-out sun
over Manchester to the east   which we can hear
as loom rumble through the steel   where buddleia
holds the signal at maroon for miles in summer
      where we time our blinks with the freight train's red lantern
so as not to miss a thing   where stones pulled up
to cast leave an empty chocolate tray in the earth
      where the great spoil banks of the motorway are seeded
and goblins weave down minor roads on mopeds
with the horsepower of sewing machines   in fishtail
parkas   where the fields brew runoff   and plinths
of concrete stand   with no discernible function
      where the night glitters in a ring around potato drills
and we are young and green in the old and afterwards
      stood out in it not knowing the storm has passed
and the first landscape of speed is gathering moss

Sparrowhawk

I'm all in. *This* I can get behind.
I'm doing my Dracula cape routine.
You look horrified. The starling's beak
opens. *Fuck, help me out here*
are the words you'd feed it. Embarrassed
to be caught in such a shameful act?
A pillow fight? A slash through the puffa?
I don't think so. Just distracted.
Your move. Stop watching me eating.
Hard to tear your gaze away
from how I'm fixed on the task in claw?
Admit it. In among your stringy ethics
you *lurve* watching a hawk like a hawk.

Adrenaline

A piece of piss to flush you out,
who put the spear in the sleeper's hand
when woken in the dark, who slams
the brake before the headlamps seize
the deer, who flash floods through a crowd,
who rises to sirens, who lives
in the river running under the moment
we think we're in, who likes it loud,
who slows the violence down for us,
who sees itself in threats, in the person
pulling a knife, who takes its cues
from the archives, too, who detonates
down the decades, fluffed to come, to scream
and hide inside a thunderous chord,
whose high season is war, who numbs
us up, whose place of worship is
the theme park, who as Pan jumped us
in antique hills and glades but plies
its trade on bright alluvial plains
these days, whose tide goes out, whose curtain
falls once test results come back
or news sinks in, whose parachute silk
is gathered up and packed when we find
ourselves crossing an inland sea
that's scarred and cracked, a caravan
surprised, who ransacks us then leaves
us high and dry, turned inside out.

Long-Eared Owl

You can feel that a bone has had some sort of use in its life
—Henry Moore

If you try to picture his spine   like where
it could be right now   tonight   like where

it could have gone   his trunk   mainframe
the thing that bore his walk and weight

you start to regurgitate
the indigestible bones of a difficult year

urgh   unmooring   pot plants next to your suitcase
         like breadfruit in the Bounty's wake
   Lime Street   Euston

urgh   leaving a man behind   a man overboard
         slowly turning into a sculpture
   fine tremors   twitches   weakness in the hand

urgh   a diagnosis with a 'motor' in it
       and a thought loosened   fluid
         from the spinal tap   an embrocation
       and next thing a thought up and running

urgh   you starting to put it all together
       the parts beginning to turn over
               and churn
          not the doctors' words
       which went in one ear   and out the other

urgh   you carrying his ready reckoner   tables of odds
       his secret system   the gambler's friend
            which also contains
         the Beaufort scale   the tides at Liverpool (Gladstone Dock)
       sines and cosines   Burgundy and Bordeaux   the years
            the major Port houses declared
       the Underground   South Kensington   Sloane Square

urgh   your first mice bristling between the rails

urgh   a woman in furs   with two Dalmatians   heaves
       into a grid   George Best   serving his ban
         standing outside the fire station   waiting for his lift
          among picturesque Punks

urgh   drinking in the Builder's   the Potter
       the Phene   so posh the urinal has a foot-guard for back-spatter

urgh   vigils   in dry baths   in halls of residence
       in camper vans   on tiled floors
         on futons and many sofas   fallen into London's
       upholstery   springs   foam   horse hair
       feathers   cellular structures
       lost coins   biros   pet fur

urgh   breaking into a burger kiosk   lighting a candle
or waiting behind a wall drape in a church niche
till everybody has finished saying their prayers

urgh   escaping on an overnight coach from Victoria   falling asleep
        to signs   Brent Cross   Flitwick   Newport Pagnell
        The North   the names of rivers in the dark
and somewhere   out there   about to be born
        the first students of your own

urgh   an eyeball   blinking through the streets
sketching anything that stays still long enough

urgh   working from the model   holding the pencil
between marks like a crucifix to a vampire

urgh   'West End Girls'   charcoal   Conté crayon
under your nails   the darkwood bank   black pens on chains
the smell of beeswax   an overdraft   the rain

urgh   washing your armpits in the etching sluice with Swarfega

urgh   stealing   pastéis de natas   spinach filos
        from Boris's   who claimed Hendrix paid a visit
the night he died   'the night he inhaled his own vomit?'

urgh   your first avocado   from Waitrose
        'put some vinegar in the hole'

urgh   seasick   your first trip abroad
        Newhaven   Dieppe   Gare du Nord
        where you copy into your sketchbook: *Mauvais souvenirs,*
        soyez pourtant les bienvenus vous êtes ma jeunesse lointaine . . .

urgh   nights ending at the bakery under Trellick Tower

urgh   fetching turps back from the builder's yard
            that does VAT receipts in elegant cursive script

urgh   being called home   making a bedside sketch
        then days of the dead   midsummer   pictures from Mexico
            on a barroom television   when replays show
                Maradona using his hand
        but the goal allowed to stand

urgh   walking everywhere   measuring distance
        in cubits   femurs   sciatic nerves
        passing the load-bearing vertebrae   of that Henry Moore
                twice a day

urgh   you Chaim Soutine at Smithfield
        sketching the meat   moving into the city

urgh   you Whistler   on the Albert Bridge
        jeans stiff with paint   half cut   dead on your feet

urgh   looking through the useful plants
        in the Physic Garden   finding nothing that would help

urgh   you in his overcoat
            when you weren't yourself

and when the owl flies away   you wonder where it goes
        if it perches in the trees   and waits

        out of mind   if it endures lean spells
        if it's always around or hereabouts

        keeping to the shadows   if it's shared
        with many   following vole booms

        cold fronts   climacterics
        longing to settle on what it is

        a shy nocturnal thing heard
        in pinewoods on summer evenings

Nightjar

gorsewhinfurzefuzzvuzzenwhinnywhin
vuzzwhinfurzegorsefurzegorsevuzzen
whinfurzegorsefurzegorsevuzzengorse
furzegorsevuzzengorsewhinnywhinvuzz
gorsewhinnywhinvuzzfurzegorsewhinny
vuzzenvuzzwhinfuzzfurzegorsevuzzen
gorsewhinfurzefuzzfurzevuzzenvuzzwhin
furzegorsewhinnynightjarfurzevuzzen
whinfurzefuzzvuzzenwhinnywhingorse
furzegorsefurzegorsevuzzenwhinnyvuzz
gorsewhinfurzegorsefurzegorsevuzzengorse
furzegorsevuzzengorsewhinnywhinvuzz
whinnywhinvuzzfurzegorsewhinnyvuzzen
whingorsefuzzvuzzvuzzenwhinnyfurze

Panic Attack, Tsukiji Market

If you get there early enough, you find
sleep's silver and bycatch before the plain
facts of the day. Before you dynamite
the coral with words, before you learn to think
like a factory ship, before you understand
the business acumen behind a shoal
display, you're a kid discovering treasure
laid out on the steps of the Agora,
under the ruined arch of Octavia,

the dead fish turning you into a time traveller,
doubly so if you're visiting jet-lagged
like here. The fish give back familiar daggers,
and even though I can't say I recall
tuna big as cling-filmed, bled-out mermen
from alien reefs, swordfish with fancy sails
or these carmine tentacles and opal claws,
I've seen this shoal that's seen it all before

before.　　　　　　　Then eels disturb the surface.
Eels alive, on a furious spin cycle,
a lubed-up cluster fuck, a vinyl
black writhing, endless, nothing the eye
can settle on, no frame, just a live feed
into the cold cabling of an underworld.

Putting the lid back on the drum, our guide
tells us how these eels were brought to market
with lamps once, to mimic the lunar phase
above a tank rocked gently from side
to side to simulate their native currents.

Breathe. Pity the mud grey sole, the humble dab,
even here, a lifetime from St John's Precinct,
and believe somebody lifts the lid to look
in on us, to see how we are doing,
and all the noises and the smells come back,
same polystyrene ruins, same frost indoors,
whetstones, oilskin aprons, slippery floors,
wherever you go, fish markets being the same,
glittering at dawn, gone by midday.

Mistle Thrush

The first park is always the fastest park,
parked under a cloudless
sky and fastened in memory
with stakes and ropes. The word *picnic*
is a tablecloth thrown onto the *grass*
attached to the word *green*.

The word *idyll* waits out of earshot.
A faun in the fountain burbles.
There is Sunblest. There is Golden Wonder.
And then, thunder.

Now the park begins bristling under that sky
which has darkened. This is the future.
This is counting towards the sound.
These are the particles rising
like the bead in your cream soda.

This is the mizzy beginning its song
from the top of the highest tree.
This is a drone shot of a thunder god.
This is a dangerous place to be

an I, sings the mizzy—I, a copper crozier.
I, a silver vaulting pole.
I, a suit of platinum armour.
I, a boom of gold.

The mizzy, with its restraining order
on humans, the wariest thrush.
The mizzy, that's working the park pretty loose.
The day is all coming unstuck.
Where a moment ago you were in a safe place
now there's distance everywhere you look.

The mizzy will only allow you so close.
The thunder follows the flash.
The words that you're learning all carry a charge
and attract or repel. Bring it on,
the mizzy sings, holding its nerve,
flying in the face of us.

Hole in the Wall

I lean in close and smell its faint bilge note.
I screen my digits but the hole in the wall
knows who I am. One time, it ate my card.

If the high street were a reef, it'd be its shark
and we'd be like those smaller fish that swim
right in to clean its teeth. And if some Hole

in the Wall Gang come and try to tear it out,
when fear moves on the waters of the reef,
it squirts a special dye and clamps up tight.

I used to go deeper into the hole
by coming here to keep an evening fed,
to stay tanked up for longer. *Would you like*

a receipt? Proof that I passed this way one night
and dived for pearls wearing a suit with lead
in my boots. *Would you like to check your balance?*

Swing

Late summer evenings in swampy clearings,
Pan's boot camp. They're ambushing themselves
again, from certain trees with boughs that wear
garters, tied-off snarls of rope
flagging up they're good to bear
a load. They've practised this for years

returning to these scrapes, this cordage
too thick for skipping games
but thinner than the type that lives
coiled up under the school stage
for tug-o'-war. Looping it round a branch
they remember a forgotten smell of tar.

The mount: nobody round here touches tyres,
forget the frilly Fragonards of art.
They're looking for the kind of stick you'd use
to push a piece of better timber through
the band-saw blade in woodwork, or
the kind for throwing to monotonous dogs,

though knotted to a tree, shuttling
between the earth and sky, a whole summer
waltzes on its axle. They queue
to jump, and practise certain styles
widely understood and recognized.
Some go silently. Others have battle cries.

Their eyes take photographs. Clouds
beneath their feet. An inclined plain
of wheat. An onlooker's shy smile
invisible at normal running speeds.
A bonfire's scat. The nettles on the dump
bumfluffed in close up. After they've jumped

most of them can't wait to go around
again, the youngest hanging back
like understudy savages,
and always one who gets his kicks
shoving first timers from the scaffold.
The tree ticks and creaks like in a church

where weeks from now they'll kneel in prayer
before an altar of spaghetti hoops,
Fray Bentos beef, pink hymnbooks packed
as tight as tinned fish in the pews, to sing
We plough the fields and scatter . . .
knowing it doesn't matter. Here

gravity can't work out where they've gone.
History isn't looking. Before
they hand the tethered baton on
and everybody in line moves up one,
they practise their escape until it's dark.
The tree records them in its rings and bark.

Curlew

On election night Pan fantasizes
about electoral reform
by picturing the high moorland
where ballot boxes go to spawn.
He's trying to remember the curlew
but it's hard—it starts strong,
wavers, bubbles, then falls towards
earth, but the timing's off, the phrasing's

wrong. Watching from a safe seat
he has fantasized about running
himself, but in heels and goat chaps
he'd likely lose his deposit.
His town is demented with counting
while its estuary always declares
rain fallen hours ago in the hills.
In the hills. There's a lag on the line.

He's gone to the country. The markets
are fluttering. He's emptied his head
of the news cycle. Helicopters
are called out to search for subjects
with a history of wandering.
Now he uses his pipe as a backscratcher.
Still the song won't come. To think
he once had the curlew by heart.

The Story of the Hangover

Once, before wild vine or maritime grain,
somebody must have noticed this, one day
in prehistory, watched how scavenging dogs
would lollop sideways from a rotten windfall,
and decided to try some; say an elder
of twenty-seven summers, calloused and worn,

his unscarred liver startled by this new,
simple poison, this blushing through the gut
the world was waiting for, its seafarers,
its herdsmen camped out on a darkened plain;
that will loosen tongues before they're barely talking,
that empires will be founded on one day;

though for now, we've a drunkard in a clearing
who doesn't know his limit, or have the words,
just a howling at the moon, his tongue on fire,
having stumbled on the biggest thing since fire,

and no one in his tribe sees the discovery:
instead, thinking him entered by wood spirits,
they lash him to a stake beyond the cave-mouth
(the first spare room), where wives and sons and daughters
keep all-night vigil through his groans and snores
and in the morning bring trepanning flints.

Positioning

Somewhere between an exhaust fitter in kitten heels
and an astrophysicist in fuck-me pumps,
if that makes sense?

Between two extremes, though we won't use the word 'extreme'.
We need to put some space between you and the snorkel parka,
between you and social housing policy.

Somewhere between a neurosurgeon in a kilt
and a dog groomer in a muumuu,
if that makes sense?

We can pretty much take this anywhere.
Remember: a brand is a promise.
If we get this right and hit those revenue streams
it'll pretty much all be down to positioning.

We need to tone down the regional accent.
We need to play up the regional accent.

Somewhere between a media buyer with a half beard
and a poet in artisanal denim,
if this is making any sense at all?

Oiks

Once, they had hearts of oik, each *bud*, each *mate*,
each *bruv* were sappy words that glued them together,
then new words came to loosen those, like solvents,
and as the cities grew, oiks could be seen
in cafes, buses, or walking oikily along
keeping their sadness to themselves, though it sang
     in the skin on a mug of coffee, the sun on high brickwork,
     in the pitch-shift of an aircraft going over;
or waiting for weekends to come around like picture cards
     in a spongy bar-room deck, looking for a kink
     in a pool cue rolled on baize and calling this wisdom

and they did all the oiky things: pointing at big buildings
as they entered the city shouldering sticks with bundles
     of ugsome clobber tied to the end, enjoying
     this simple leverage, saying 'God bless Dick Whittington',
and finding rented lodgings above mobile phone outlets,
having all the makings of home about their persons,
     typically: toothbrush, steel comb, two pouches of counterfeit
     tobacco, roll-on deodorant, ancestral gall stone,
and these and other possibles were laid on the candlewick
like a full kit inspection or a shakedown in those bridewells

they left off their CVs before starting on Mondays,
before breaking their promises to the man with the keys
about leaving it like they found it, true to form,
     and nobody considered the oiks alone

on their first nights, too frightened to go out and explore,
switching the oik-box on to take blue communion
with every other oik in oik-lodgings all over old oik-land
where oik was spoken and oikiness general.

Treecreeper

On the telegraph post
　　that weeps creosote
　　　　and gathers a moss
　　as it once did in life,

on a mast that's played host
　　to the corposant
　　　　and creaks in a gale
　　as it once did in life,

on the flagpole that stands
　　in a rootstock of stone
　　　　and flies the colours
　　as it once did in life,

see the treecreeper's ghost
　　as it spirals and probes
　　　　and finds our blindside
　　as it once did in life.

Quadrat

After the disaster he went to inspect
a certain patch of rock between the tides.
Oiled guillemots were getting all the headlines,
barrels of ink being spent on their black feathers

while limpets and sea snails went by the by,
the small print of the shoreline. Big surf boomed
and echoed off the stacks. He scratched four corners
to make a window on a glassy mudstone

and started counting what was clinging on there
in summer, when it baked blue at low water,
in winter, when it shone glossy as the ravens
that hijacked one another in the wind,

heading home to tabulate the numbers
in a kitchen where a Rayburn and a storm lamp
provided light and shelter enough for study.
A slow newsroom. The scholar's habitat.

No crossword, horoscope, or game of chess
on the beach with Death, or even noughts and crosses,
just a census of who lives at one address,
what's happening in the constellation Quadrat,

no op-ed column or gastropod gossip
of mantled ears pressed to the world's wall,
just the act of having drawn a line around things
and a willingness to take whatever's found there,

the spill long having sailed the front pages
and dispersed into the archives and the footnotes,
and why he stuck it no one knew, until one day
he handed on his solar paper round

to a poet. Big mistake. I've let things slide.
The data set crumbled while I stayed home
to polish the words. The window washed away.
And that was the last entry, and this is the poem.

Gannet

for J.H.

Starved on a diet of distance,
of optic specks and crumbs,
but snarled in monofilament
one flapping bird becomes
a feast in close-up—blue
kohled eyes, sharp carbon-steel
beak—till one of us threw
their coat over, and it fell still.

A blacked-out budgerigar
denied the basic privileges
of cuttlebone and mirror
dreams of colonial perches
and pigeons shelved in lofts
survive the darkness system
by picturing the lost
cliff roosts that once held them.

Sightseers film the event:
us cutting free a bird.
The pictures are being sent
to social platforms, shared
and liked. Samurai swan
tempered far out to sea,
you can look now, we've all gone
back to our sad gannetry.

Saturday

This whole long-lagging, muzzy, mizly morning . . .
—Samuel Taylor Coleridge

Every day is Saturday.
We wake slowly, unhitched from the week.
A plane drones high above the house.
The post comes late. Monday has gone,
its inch-deep sheets of rainwater
on bus shelter roofs, its faces below
that gaze into the day before last,
its kids in playgrounds forming up
and filing through the unchained doors.
Tuesday is nowhere to be found,
the week's waiting room with its magazines
called *Saturday*, its tongue and groove,
its dinnertimes and post office queues.
Wednesday, half closing day, has drawn
the shutters down on itself, the midweek
sump, its skiver's moon, its halfway
point and cigarette break round the back.
You remember Thursday? Its rentman's knock,
its pint after work, its lolling asleep
on a stranger's shoulder on the last bus.
Though Friday, for all its faults, still stands
in the memory as the triumphal arch
into Saturday, till they knock it down.
The working week gone west, cut loose

like a city from its port. But wait:
we're missing our day of rest, and can't
even bring ourselves to say its name.
Every Saturday used to end. Then came
a whining vacuum, a muzzy head,
deserted streets. We rise in praise.
Give thanks. That nightmare is over. All
our tomorrows will be Saturdays.

Great Black-Backed Gull

The tide keeps bringing everything you need.
The tip is like a slowed down sea to gulls
who trawl behind the trucks or dip in strong
kinking glides above the ribbons and shreds
of dross, the spume and swell.
                                        Taken to see *Jaws*
at the ABC, the robot great white shark
made us jump, but later came the slower thought
of real great whites cruising the seas of the world
while I lay in bed. *What we are dealing with here*
is a perfect engine, an eating machine . . .

Now, a landfill lubber with binoculars,
I pick out great blacks from the smaller gulls
above the waste where, fathoms deep, the shark
still swims among the wreckage of who we were
forty summers ago. They're such powerful birds
and the tide keeps bringing everything they need.

Beach

It was one thing to visit them, to follow the file of people from the
car park down onto the beach, a half mile to the scene, though
even with the tape and media it wasn't like a crime, more a sand
fair, or a circus if the big top had blown away in a gritty wind and
all the animals had died, leaving a sweet scent under a big sky, the
attraction of scale, a sudden sacred landscape of soft monoliths
you couldn't get your head round, the circling and approach
from every angle by souvenir hunters with their hacksaws like
leaf-cutters in a two-lane ant line, the protesters who'd been with
aerosols and defiled their flanks or spoken truth to power—take
your pick—and the dogs mad with discovering the big stink at
the centre of the universe,

and it was another to crawl inside one, past the clickbait teeth
and under the fatberg head, into the chambers of a gut as slow
to cool as a furnace bed, and so a snug—if greasy—shelter, lit by
your phone with no signal, all purely voluntary, no lots having
been cast or storm endured at sea, seeking to get as far as possible
from being a core customer, from traditional big players and broad
narratives, a place outside arborescent hierarchies and the general
drift towards consumer-driven content, to spend a night imagining
dives, going deep, falling eventually into a single cycle of sleep and
a lonely sonar dream, sensing daybreak from the gull-fest outside,
a faint commotion through the walls of meat, and with no need to
tickle any ribs, or set fire to the coracle you didn't bring, emerge
un-spat back into the day, the world exactly how you left it.

ACKNOWLEDGEMENTS

Many thanks to the editors of *Areté*, *Eighteen Bridges*, *London Review of Books*, *The New Yorker*, *The Poetry Review*, *The Times Literary Supplement* and *Wild Court*, where some of these poems have previously been published.

'The Sloth' first appeared in the pamphlet *Cold Vision* (Hexham Book Festival); 'Gentian Violet' was commissioned by the Arden Bloomsbury Shakespeare 400 project (in response to Sonnet 99) and included in *On Shakespeare's Sonnets* (Bloomsbury); 'Positioning' was written at the invitation of Catherine Marcangeli/ Bluecoat on the fiftieth anniversary of *The Mersey Sound*; 'Saturday' accompanied the photographs of Tom Wood in *Termini* (Éditions GwinZegal); 'Moss' was written for Colin Riley's song cycle *In Place*; and 'Great Black-Backed Gull' has been recycled from Tim Dee's book *Landfill* (Little Toller).

'Quadrat' is loosely founded on Richard Pearce's long observations, and I'm grateful to him for our visit to Porth Mear on the north Cornish coast. 'Moorhen' owes a debt to Colin Tudge's *The Day Before Yesterday*.

I'm grateful to Matt Haw, Warren Mortimer, Carole Romaya, Kate VerSprill, and my editor, Don Paterson.